Dream big, our little Boo

— Mommy & Daddy —

Copyright © 2023 by Yeonsil Yoo.

All rights reserved. No part of this book may be reproduced or transmitted
in any form or by any means, electronic or mechanical, including photocopying,
recording, or by any information storage and retrieval system,
without prior written permission from the copyright holder.

www.upflybooks.com

Paperback: 978-1-7388188-0-8
eBook PDF: 978-1-7388188-1-5
Hardcover: 978-1-7388188-2-2

My First Trip to Korea
나의 첫 한국 여행

Made with ❤ by Upfly Books

Written by Yeonsil Yoo | Illustrated by Anastasiya Halionka

"Yay! School is over!"
"야호! 학교 끝!"

Summer vacation has started at Yoona's school.
유나 학교에 여름 방학이 시작되었어요.

Yoona is excited to play
with her favorite toys every day at home.
유나는 좋아하는 장난감을 가지고 매일 집에서
놀 생각을 하니 신이 났어요.

"Do you like summer vacation?" Mommy asks.
"방학 시작하니까 좋아?" 엄마가 물었어요.

"Yeah! Vacation is the best!"
"응! 방학이 제일 좋아!"

"Why do you like vacation? What do you want to do?"
Mommy looks at Yoona curiously.
"방학이 왜 좋아? 뭐하고 싶은데?"
엄마는 궁금해하며 유나를 쳐다봤어요.

Every day I can watch TV,
매일 TV도 보고,

eat ice cream,
아이스크림도 먹고,

and play with Fishy and T-rex!
물고기랑 공룡이랑 놀 수 있잖아!

Oh, and Ducky as well!
아, 오리도!

"But Yoona, you can play with your toys any time.
This summer, why don't we go to Korea?
"그런데 유나야, 장난감 가지고 노는 건 언제든지 할 수 있잖아.
이번 여름에는 한국에 가는 건 어때?

You can try a summer camp in Korea and meet new friends there!"
한국에서 여름 캠프에 가면 새로운 친구들도 만날 수 있어!"

"No! I don't want new friends!" Yoona shouts.
"싫어! 난 새로운 친구들 싫어!" 유나가 소리쳤어요.

"Then, what about visiting Grandma and Grandpa? If we go to Korea, we can visit and play with Grandma, Grandpa, Aunt, and Uncle."
Mommy talks softly while she holds Yoona's hands.
"그러면 할머니, 할아버지 댁에 가는 건? 한국에 가면, 할머니랑 할아버지랑 이모랑 이모부랑 같이 놀 수 있어."
엄마가 유나 손을 잡으며 이야기했어요.

"I miss Grandma and Grandpa..."
"할머니, 할아버지는 보고 싶어..."

Yoona wants to visit and play with Grandma, Grandpa, Aunt, and Uncle, but she doesn't want to make new friends.
유나는 할머니, 할아버지, 이모, 이모부랑 같이 놀고 싶었지만, 새로운 친구들을 사귀는 건 싫었어요.

On the plane to Korea, Yoona looks out the window.
한국으로 가는 비행기에서 유나는 창 밖을 내다봤어요.

Big, fluffy clouds are everywhere,
and all the houses and cars under the clouds look so tiny.
They look like her toys at home.
몽글몽글한 큰 구름이 여기저기 있고,
구름 아래 모든 집과 차들이 아주 조그맣게 보였어요.
집에 있는 장난감처럼요.

But she can't stop thinking about the camp in Korea
Mommy was talking about.
하지만 유나는 엄마가 이야기했던
한국 여름 캠프가 계속 생각났어요.

'What if no one wants to play with me?'
'아무도 나랑 놀아주지 않으면 어떡하지?'

'I can't speak Korean well. What if the other kids make fun of me?
I just want to stay at home and watch TV every day!'
'나는 한국말도 잘 못하는데. 다른 애들이 나 놀리면 어떡하지?
그냥 매일 집에서 TV나 보고 싶다!'

After a long flight, the plane lands in Korea.
오랫동안 비행기를 타고, 드디어 한국에 도착했어요.

At the airport, Grandma, Grandpa, Aunt, and Uncle
welcome Yoona with big hugs.
공항에는 할머니, 할아버지, 이모, 이모부가
유나를 껴안아주며 반겨주었어요.

Although Yoona has chatted with them through video calls so many times,
she is too shy to say "Annyeong ha se yo" ("hello" in Korean).
So she just hides behind Mommy.
그동안 유나는 화상 통화로 많이 이야기했지만,
'안녕하세요'라고 얘기하는 게 부끄러웠어요.
그래서 엄마 뒤에 숨어 버렸어요.

Aunt and Uncle give Yoona lots of toys, and Grandma and Grandpa spoil her with so many yummy ice creams and snacks. Yoona is so happy with all of these gifts and goodies.
이모랑 이모부는 장난감도 많이 주셨고, 할머니랑 할아버지는 맛있는 아이스크림과 과자를 많이 사주셨어요. 유나는 이런 선물들을 받아 너무 행복했어요.

"Is it delicious, Yoona?" Grandma asks.
"유나야 맛있어?" 할머니가 물었어요.

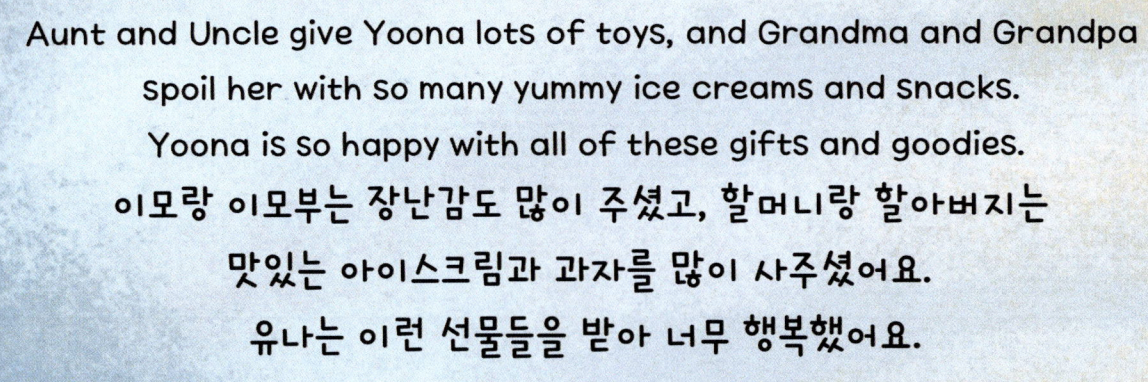

"Yeah, it's so yummy! I love ice cream! But Grandma, don't tell Mommy! Mommy said I shouldn't eat too much ice cream!"
Yoona speaks in a whispering voice to Grandma.
"응 맛있어! 나는 아이스크림 너무 좋아! 그런데 할머니, 엄마한테는 말하지 마세요! 엄마가 아이스크림 많이 먹지 말랬어!"
유나가 조용히 할머니에게 속삭였어요.

"Okay, this is our secret!" Grandma says, with a big smile.
"알았어! 이건 우리 비밀!" 할머니가 활짝 웃으며 대답했어요.

Yoona slowly decides that she will like visiting Korea.
유나는 점점 한국에 오는 게 좋다고 생각했어요.

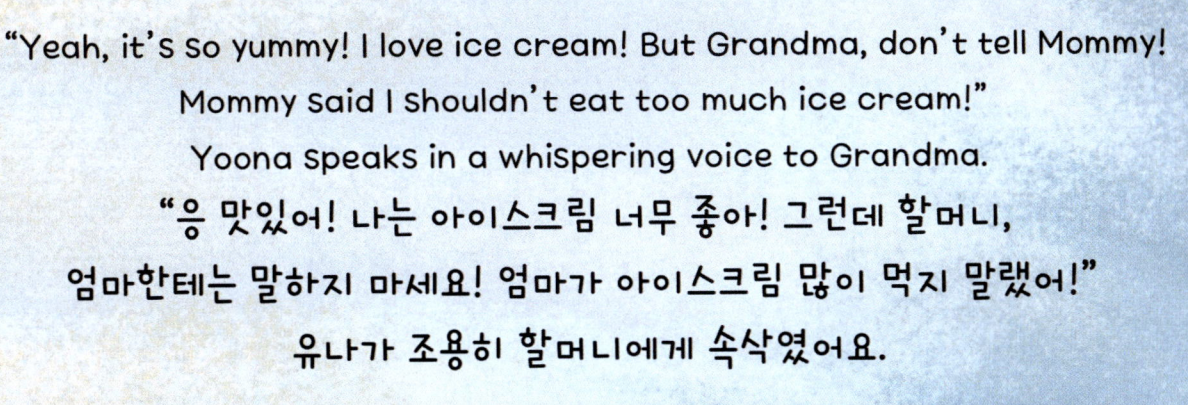

But whenever Mommy talks about the summer camp,
Yoona becomes worried.
하지만 엄마가 여름 캠프 이야기를 꺼낼 때마다,
유나는 걱정이 밀려왔어요.

"Yoona, we're going to visit the new camp tomorrow.
There will be lots of games to play, fun books and toys!
And you can make new friends and meet the teachers!"
Mommy seems excited, but Yoona is upset.
"유나야, 우리 내일부터 여름 캠프 갈 거야.
거기 가면 재미있는 게임이랑, 책이랑, 장난감도 많이 있어!
그리고 새로운 친구들이랑 선생님도 만날 수 있고!"
엄마는 신나서 이야기했지만, 유나는 화났어요.

"I told you, I don't wanna go to the new camp!" Yoona shouts.
"내가 얘기했잖아, 난 여름 캠프 가기 싫어!"
유나가 소리쳤어요.

"Why not?"
"왜 싫어?"

"If I go to the camp, T-rex will be alone at Grandma's house.
I'm going to stay home and play with T-rex!"
Yoona looks down at the floor, trying to hold back her tears.
"내가 캠프 가면 공룡은 할머니 집에 혼자 있잖아!
난 집에서 공룡이랑 놀 거야!"
유나는 바닥을 바라보며 눈물을 참았어요.

"T-rex won't be alone. Mommy will be there with him."
Mommy talks gently to Yoona while she rubs Yoona's back.
"공룡은 혼자 있지 않을 거야. 엄마가 옆에 있어줄게."
엄마가 유나 등을 쓸어주며 조용히 이야기했어요.

"No! I don't like it! I don't like the camp
and the new friends!" Yoona cries.
"그래도 싫어! 난 새 캠프도, 새 친구들도 싫어!"
유나가 울음을 터트렸어요.

Mommy scooches down and holds Yoona's hands to comfort her.
엄마는 쪼그려 앉아 유나 손을 잡으며 달랬어요.

"Yoona, we haven't even tried yet, right?
If you don't like it after you try it tomorrow,
you don't have to go anymore.
But you need to at least give it a try. Deal?"
"유나야, 우리 아직 안 가봤지?
내일 가보고 싫으면 그다음부터는 안 가도 돼.
하지만 적어도 한 번은 가보고 결정하자. 어때?"

"Okay..." Yoona reluctantly nods.
"알았어..." 유나는 어쩔 수 없이 고개를 끄덕였어요.

Finally, it is the first day of summer camp.
드디어 오늘은 여름 캠프에 가는 첫날이에요.

Yoona drags herself around the entire morning,
hoping to avoid going to the camp.
유나는 캠프에 가지 않기를 바라면서
아침 내내 시간을 질질 끌었어요.

"Yoona, you should hurry up and change your clothes!"
"유나 빨리 옷 갈아입어야 돼!"

"Okay…"
"응…"

Yoona answers reluctantly,
but she is still rolling around the floor, doing nothing.
유나는 마지못해 대답했지만,
바닥에 뒹굴거리며 아무것도 하지 않았어요.

Soon, Mommy enters her room.
잠시 후 엄마가 유나 방에 들어왔어요.

"Yoona, you haven't changed yet?
Can you change your clothes, please, right now?"
Mommy is very upset.
"유나, 아직도 옷 안 갈아입은 거야?
지금 빨리 갈아입을래?" 엄마는 엄청 화가 났어요.

"Okay... I'm changing..."
"알았어... 갈아입고 있어..."

Yoona sighs and starts to change her clothes, one piece at a time.
유나는 한숨을 푹 쉬며 옷을 주섬주섬 하나씩 입기 시작했어요.

Mommy, Daddy, and Yoona arrive at the school.
One teacher greets them with a big smile.
엄마랑 아빠랑 유나가 학교에 도착했어요.
그러자 한 선생님이 미소 지으며 반겨주셨어요.

"You must be Yoona. Welcome to our class!"
"네가 유나구나. 여름 캠프에 온 것을 환영해!"

Yoona becomes even more nervous:
unlike back home in Canada, everyone here is speaking only Korean.
유나는 더욱 긴장했어요. 캐나다와는 달리, 모두들 한국말을 했으니까요.

But the teacher continues talking.
"Let's say bye-bye to Mommy and Daddy,
and then I'll introduce you to the other kids in the class!"
하지만 선생님은 계속 이야기했어요.
"엄마랑 아빠한테 인사하자,
그러면 선생님이 같은 반 친구들 소개해줄게!"

Yoona sends Mommy and Daddy a signal by shaking her head subtly,
but Mommy and Daddy don't seem to notice.
유나는 고개를 내저으며 엄마랑 아빠한테 신호를 보냈지만,
엄마랑 아빠는 눈치채지 못한 것 같았어요.

"Have fun!" Mommy and Daddy cheer.
"재밌게 보내!" 엄마랑 아빠가 소리쳤어요.

In the classroom, some of the kids are already chatting, laughing, and running around.
교실에는 몇몇 아이들이 벌써 이야기하고, 웃고, 뛰어다니고 있었어요.

When Yoona enters the classroom, everyone looks at her.
유나가 교실에 들어가니 모두들 유나를 쳐다봤어요.

Yoona tries not to look at anybody.
유나는 아무도 쳐다보지 않으려고 했어요.

She walks towards some of the toys and picks up a yellow digger toy.
그리고는 장난감이 있는 쪽으로 걸어가 노란색 포크레인을 집어 들었어요.

Her classmates want to talk to her,
but no one is willing to be the first one.
친구들 역시 다가가서 이야기하고 싶었지만
먼저 선뜻 나서는 아이는 없었어요.

Then, one boy walks over to Yoona.
그때 한 아이가 유나에게 다가갔어요.

"Hi, my name is Minwoo. What's your name?"
"안녕, 내 이름은 민우야. 네 이름은 뭐니?"

"I'm Yoona."
"나는 유나."

Minwoo beams with joy and continues to talk to Yoona.
민우가 활짝 웃으며 유나에게 말했어요.

"Do you like diggers? I like them, too!
There's a big yellow digger toy at the play center.
Do you want to go and play together?"
"너도 포크레인 좋아해? 나도 좋아하는데!
저쪽 놀이 센터에 가면 훨씬 더 큰 포크레인 있는데
같이 가서 놀래?"

"YEAH!"
"응!"

Yoona and Minwoo hold hands,
and together they run to the play center.
유나랑 민우는 손잡고 놀이 센터 쪽으로 뛰어갔어요.

And just like Minwoo said, there was
a big, yellow digger toy in the play center.
놀이 센터에는 정말 민우가 말한 대로
노란색 큰 포크레인 장난감 차가 있었어요.

"Let's go! Let's hop on it together!"
"가자! 우리 같이 타자!"

Yoona and Minwoo run to the digger.
유나랑 민우는 포크레인 쪽으로 달려갔어요.

While she was having so much fun playing with Minwoo,
Yoona thought to herself,
민우와 함께 재밌게 놀면서 유나는 생각했어요.

'Playing with Minwoo is so much fun!
I can't wait to come back tomorrow!'
'민우랑 노는 건 너무 재밌다! 내일 또 와야지!'

Have you ever been worried or scared about something, before you even tried it?

혹시 시도해보기도 전에 혼자 걱정하고 무서워한 적 있나요?

Sometimes we can be scared of places we've never been, and people who are very different.

때로는 우리가 가보지 않은 곳이나,
우리와 다른 사람들이 두렵게 느껴질 때가 있어요.

But when we get to know them,
we find out that there is nothing to be scared or worried about.
하지만 조금씩 알아 가다 보면,
전혀 무서워하거나 걱정할 필요가 없다는 것을 알게 될 거예요.

So, next time you are scared about something new,
why don't you give it a try first, and see what happens?
그러니 다음번에 새로운 것이 무섭게 느껴진다면,
먼저 한번 해보고 어떤 일이 벌어지는지 보는 건 어떨까요?

Bonus!

Download printable
vocabulary flashcards for FREE!

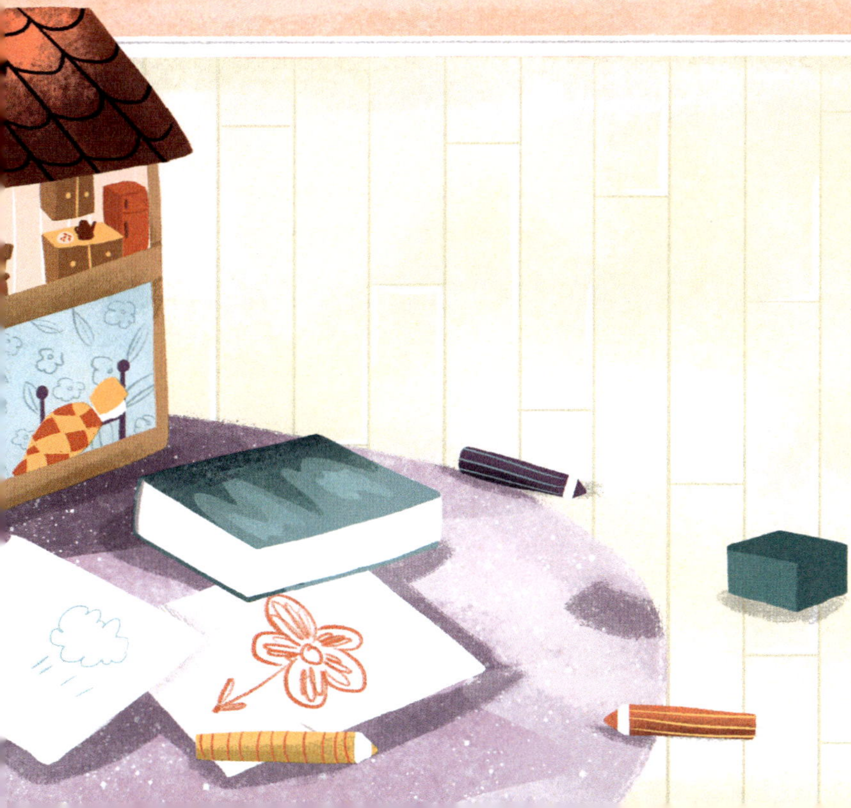

If you enjoy this book, please share your thoughts on Amazon! It will help other families like you discover this book, and will allow me to keep creating exciting adventures to share with everyone!

About the author

Yeonsil is a children's author and proud mother of a multicultural child who is Korean, Chinese, American, and Canadian.

Yeonsil is passionate about giving her daughter the chance to connect with her family roots and embrace her diverse background.

As the author of the 'My First Trip' series,
Yeonsil aims to provide children with fun and meaningful stories that help them explore the world's cultures and be proud of their origins.

For more information, and to keep updated with her books, visit her website at www.upflybooks.com or follow her on Instagram @upflybooks.

Made in the USA
Las Vegas, NV
27 September 2023